The Book for People Who Do Too Much

OTHER BOOKS BY BRADLEY TREVOR GREIVE

The Blue Day Book
The Blue Day Journal and Directory
Dear Mom
Looking for Mr. Right
The Meaning of Life
The Incredible Truth About Mothers
Tomorrow
Priceless: The Vanishing Beauty of a Fragile Planet

The Book for People Who Do Too Much

BRADLEY TREVOR GREIVE

**Andrews McMeel
Publishing**

Kansas City

05 06 07 08 TWP 10 9 8 7 6 5 4

ISBN: 0-7407-4183-7

Library of Congress Control Number: 2003113277

Book design by Holly Camerlinck

Attention: Schools and Businesses

Andrews McMeel books are available at quantity discounts with bulk purchase for educational, business, or sales promotional use. For information, please write to: Special Sales Department, Andrews McMeel Publishing, 4520 Main Street, Kansas City, Missouri 64111.

PHOTO CREDITS

Auscape International (Sydney)
www.auscape.com.au

Australian Picture Library (Sydney)
www.australianpicturelibrary.com.au

Austral International (Sydney)
www.australphoto.com.au

Sharon Beals (USA)
© Sharon Beals/ChronicleBooks.com

Norvia Behling (USA)
www.foxhillphoto.com

BIG Australia (Sydney)
www.bigaustralia.com.au

Bradley Trevor Greive (Sydney)
www.btgstudios.com

Frans Lanting Photography (USA)
www.lanting.com

Getty Images (Sydney)
www.gettyimages.com

Images on the Wildside (USA)
www.denverbryan.com

Larry Kornhak (USA)
lvk@ifas.ufl.edu

Kim Levin (USA)
www.barkandsmile.com

Photolibrary.com (Sydney)
www.photolibrary.com

Ron Kimball Studios (USA)
www.ronkimballstock.com

Stock Photos (Sydney)
www.stockphotos.com.au

Toni Tucker (USA)
www.tonitucker.com

Universal Pictorial Press & Agency (UK)
www.uppa.co.uk

Robert Williams (USA)

Detailed page credits for the remarkable photographers whose work appears in
The Book for People Who Do Too Much and other books by Bradley Trevor Greive
are freely available at www.btgstudios.com.

*"The fox knows many things,
but the hedgehog knows one big thing."*

Archilochus, 700 BC

For the hedgehogs

Acknowledgments

I always tried to do too much until a run of delightfully dramatic accidents had me laced into revealing hospital pajamas for quite some time. I've certainly learned a valuable lesson or two from my painful experience with excessive endeavor, and I am very grateful for the tremendous support that made it possible for me to share some important insights with you in this amusing little book, which I hope will entertain and enlighten you.

Considering that several drafts were completed while I was still heavily sedated, I am even more indebted than usual to my principal editors, Christine Schillig of Andrews McMeel Publishing (USA) and Jane Palfreyman of Random House (Australia). My team at BTG Studios rose to the challenge as always, and I especially want to acknowledge my executive assistant, Anita Arnold, along with photography consultant, Nick Green, both of whom toiled without pause to get my little book into production.

The Book for People Who Do Too Much relies heavily on outstanding photographs, and I am very grateful to the contributing photographers and their agents. I urge everyone interested in these images to visit www.btgstudios.com for their creators' updated contact information.

It seems like only yesterday when my esteemed literary agent, Albert J. Zuckerman of Writers House New York, sat on the edge of my hospital bed offering me timeless wisdom and considerable cheer. One of the gems he offered up was an inspiring story about the lean literary times during the late '50s and early '60s when

Al turned to Hollywood to keep his fortunes afloat. Luckily, the tanned, muscled torso he had won from years of heavy excavation in the Sudan snared him the role of Kirk Douglas's body double in *Spartacus* the minute he stepped onto the Universal Studios lot. Keen to make the most of his break, Al snuck back into the casting session again and again until he had secured similar honors for Laurence Olivier, Peter Ustinov, and a svelte Tony Curtis. Thus, in the course of one day's shooting, he was forced to gain or shed up to eighty pounds—sometimes in the same scene! When principle photography finally wrapped, Al was barely breathing and had developed a pathological fear of sandals. He crawled away to New York vowing never to put himself through such an ordeal again.

"Bradley, my boy," he advised as I lay wreathed in abrasive hospital linen and intrusive postoperative tubes, "I believe we were put on this earth to do a lot less than we think." Truer words were never spoken.

Do you feel pooped?

Do you occasionally get piercing headaches behind your right eye?

Do you bore your friends to death by going on and on and on about how much work you have to do?

And have you been so rushed or run down that your
personal grooming and general appearance have deteriorated

to the point where your friends politely avert their eyes
when you enter a room?

The good news is there are only two possible explanations
for these alarming symptoms: You have contracted a horrific
mystery disease for which there is no possible cure

or, and this is only marginally better, you are one of those people who are simply doing way too much.

Doing too much has always been a serious problem. It's no coincidence that most heart attacks occur at 9 a.m. on Monday morning. (So much for the masochistic maxim "Hard work never killed anyone.")

12   Excessive endeavor has also been known to cause premature hair loss

and commonly induces explosive indigestion along with other
painful disorders that prevent the sufferer from sitting cross-legged
or wearing fashionable vinyl pants.

Some highly motivated people of questionable intelligence deliberately do too much, but most of us gradually end up in this situation without even knowing how we got there.

One day, no matter how hard you try, you can't get through everything you wanted to accomplish without working well into the night.

The fact is that even the most polite, unassuming,

timid little creature can, after a few nights without adequate sleep,

become an absolute monster! 17

Little things soon start to drive you crazy,

and you suddenly turn on people who don't deserve it.

Simple tasks get way out of hand as mix-ups
and mess-ups start to multiply.

It becomes a huge mental struggle to haul yourself
through to the weekend,

looking forward to nothing more than just collapsing in a heap,
too tired to dream.

When we do run head-long-slam-bang into
the invisible barrier that is genuine exhaustion of body and soul,
the smart thing to do is stop and revive.

However, some folk will try any quick-fix available to keep on truckin'. Most start with a refreshing beverage loaded with sugar and caffeine or, for the more discerning palate, a cup of expensive herbal tea.

When the short-term value of these pick-me-ups is fully spent,
they may try alternative remedies such as invigorating scalp massage,

extreme Jacuzzi,

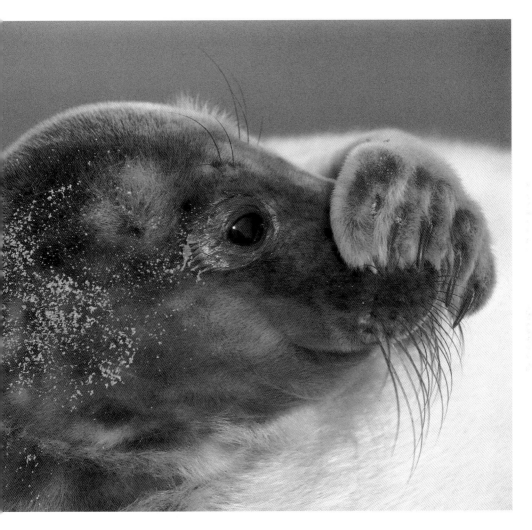

and eye-wateringly pungent aromatherapy.

As fatigue increases, newer and more powerful kick-starts will be required to maintain forward momentum.

Some desperate individuals even turn to medicinal supplements,
legal and otherwise, to fire up their failing systems. 29

This actually works wonders, although the effect can best be described as "The lights are on, but nobody's home."

Exotic pills and potions may relieve your *desire* for rest
but they will not remove your genuine *need* for rest.
The battle that rages within can seriously scramble your brain

and, in extreme cases, your head will explode!

Fascinating though such oddly destructive behavior is,
more interesting still is the fundamental question behind it all:
Why do people do too much?

The obvious answer is because there's so much to do!
If you haven't noticed, there's a lot going on in the modern world.

In the midst of it all, we are driven by a few typically human motivations.
For starters, we all want to live well. It's only natural to desire
some of the finer things in life for ourselves and those we care about. 35

We also want to leave our mark on the world.
We want to know that our life matters,
that we make a difference somehow.

Perhaps the most powerful motivation is that we want to be liked for
who we truly are. In fact, whether we admit it or not,
being liked is incredibly important to just about everybody.

Thus, even if someone wants us to do something
that seriously puts our nose out of joint,

most of the time we just offer a painfully weak smile and mumble,
"Of course, I'd be delighted."

40   Before you know it, you're knee-deep in someone else's dirty laundry;

you're baby-sitting for the third weekend in a row;

and you've become a twenty-four-hour taxi service for
family, friends, colleagues, and neighbors.

We know in our hearts that the greatest reward in life comes
from giving the greatest service to the greatest number of people.

We also know that if we don't get a move on, we will soon be left behind.
If that happens, we won't be able to provide our loved ones

with much of anything.

Together, these somewhat conflicting attitudes drive us to get to the front of the line and stay there by whatever means necessary.

Day in day out, we tirelessly sniff out opportunities to get ahead,
scrambling into position to claim what's ours,

and then it happens: Suddenly you are in the right place
at the right time, and it pays off in a big way!

Or does it?
Failure plays a part in every great success story,
but not everyone can appreciate this.

Foremost on our minds is the humiliation of defeat.
No one wants to look like a loser.

The pressure is then increased to not only keep our eye on the ball
at all times, which is stressful enough,

but, we also want to look successful, no matter what. Keeping up appearances can easily become an exhausting full-time job in itself!

Once you become obsessed with superficial symbols of success,
you tend to need more and more of them.
The world soon becomes a giant mail-order catalog.

"I want a bigger house filled with the newest new things
and the oldest antiques!"

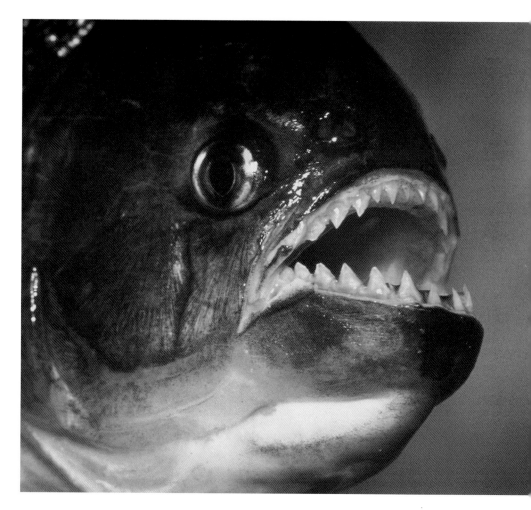

To get this stuff you must obey the creepy inner voice that says,
"Work harder, work longer, do more, earn more, have more, be more!"

Pretty soon you're eating high-energy snacks on the run;
sitting down for meals becomes a thing of the past.

You think about your responsibilities, schedules, and objectives constantly.

In fact, you can't stop thinking about them no matter how hard you try!

Even when you finally fall asleep,
your mind keeps turning over and over and over.

You know that a system that rewards committed self-destruction
will eventually chew you up and spit you out,

but you still won't slow down because you are absolutely certain
that if you take your foot off the accelerator for even a moment, 59

60 everything and everyone around you will immediately grind to a halt.

To make matters worse, the competition is always right on your tail and drawing closer by the minute. You'll have to lift your knees rather rapidly if you want to keep them a safe distance behind you.

It's enough to make you attempt the impossible.
Which, believe it or not, actually turns out to be impossible!

Before you know it, you're going down in the worst way.
You're overwhelmed, and you know it.

At this point, you'll notice two distinctly different attitudes among those around you: Some people will rub their greasy little mittens together with glee. Your demise represents an exciting opportunity for them.

Your true friends sense an opportunity, too, a chance to finally say, "Whoa, slow down. Take a breather and decide what your health and happiness are really worth."

66 A few people listen to this and change for the better, but most don't.

Some even feel angry with their friends and family for trying to help. They feel they are being held back, and if they could just be left alone to get the job done, it would be a whole lot better for all concerned.

Our admiration of heroic individual endeavor is based on some pretty inspiring precedents. Going solo and pushing through fatigue in extreme situations has saved lives and changed the course of history.

But the belief that imitating this noble behavior is necessary to get ahead in normal life or survive another day at the office is not remotely courageous. It's actually kind of stupid.

Even if such ruthless focus gets you across the finish line first,
you won't be able to enjoy the moment if there's no one
to reflect your joy or celebrate with you.

A world without hugs is not a place you want to be.

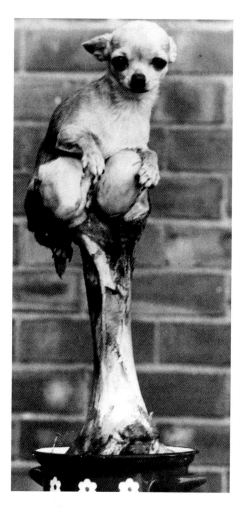

There are many so-called successful people in this sad situation. They have
72 everything they ever wanted, yet somehow, it's not nearly enough,

and a strange unfillable emptiness develops deep inside their heart.

Their personal lives may appear fine to onlookers, but they suffer badly. What once were fulfilling relationships become artificial routines.

Real passion fled the scene long ago. It's such a shame. 75

The only way to avoid this situation is to say "No!" to the hundreds of requests and demands that are more than you can handle or, frankly, aren't worth a generous slice of the one lifetime you have been given.

Most people just can't do this. As soon as someone asks for a favor they automatically say yes. They think it's a sign of strength and affection to respond with a confident "Sure, no problem!"

In fact, it's really a sign of weakness that will ultimately damage their friendships.

They're only setting themselves up to let someone down and, conversely, they'll eventually resent their friends for burdening them in the first place. Both parties soon start to question the foundations of the relationship.

So when someone special turns up with a request or an opportunity they think is perfect for you, and you get that sinking feeling as you prepare to agree to whatever they want—pause—and slowly fill your lungs with heartfelt honesty.

Then say, "Hey, you matter to me and I want to do the right thing,
but if I take this on, I will have to sacrifice something else.
So please tell me, how important is this, really?"

Take some time to consider the ramifications of your various options.
Don't be rushed into anything, and if you don't feel good about it,
be prepared to communicate this with gentle clarity.

To a close friend, you might say, "I'm so sorry. I feel terrible, but I'm just too busy to do this justice. So for now, I'll have to say no." For people who just don't appreciate your time, you may need something a little stronger, such as:

"Look, I'm already so overcommitted that I couldn't take this on without growing four more arms, a third leg, and a second head. To be honest, I've got enough fashion challenges as it is."

Finally, for serial pests, there is the foolproof cavalcade of no's,
which goes something like this: "No, no, no no, no, no, no, no, no, no,
noooooooooooooooooo thank you very much. Have a nice day!"
(This is particularly effective when delivered in a classical operatic style.)

The bottom line is that people who do too much end up doing too little of what really matters. They spend their lives buzzing from
one tiring and trivial task to another,

instead of living their dreams.

In the end it all comes down to priorities,
which sounds complicated but really isn't.

Life priorities are as basic as understanding that if you use up all your precious time and creative energy doing one thing,

you won't have much left for anything else.

Obviously, then, it makes sense to focus your time and energy
on those things that really make you feel ecstatic,
or at least happy, to be alive.

Don't take someone else's word for what those things should be.
Follow your heart to the source of that which refreshes your soul
and drink deeply from it.

If you do this, your world will become a lot bigger,
and your problems will seem significantly smaller.

You will finally be able to lighten up

and take a load off without feeling guilty or anxious.

Take some time to appreciate the inner beauty and purpose that is often forgotten in the rush-hour frenzy.

Watch the stress lines fade

and enjoy the kind of peaceful sleep
that you haven't experienced for a very, very long time.

Pretty soon, you'll feel a tingle from your nose to
your toes as you start to revive.

And when you get the spring back into your step, launch yourself
into all the things you've been putting off for all the wrong reasons.

Rediscover the simple pleasures you have been too busy
or too self-absorbed to enjoy.

Start by making room in your life for a puppy.

Learn to navigate by the stars.

Revive the lost art of conversation.

Practice your kissing

and bathe in the innocent bliss of daydreams.

Just choose to do the things that make you the sort of person
you really want to hang out with.

It's a pleasant surprise for most people
to discover that everything tastes better,

your friends are more fun,

the sky is bluer,

and the ones you love are even more beautiful

when you feel great about yourself.

If you can just say "No" with polite, unshakable conviction to anything
or anyone that would ultimately take away from all that you are,

but still maintain your compassion and understanding
for those who genuinely need your strength and friendship,

then you can look out upon a universe of wonders waiting to be discovered and enjoyed by you and those dearest to your heart

and say, "Yes!"

In memory of Biff,
a furry friend to the end